KICKBOXING AND MMA

Mastering the Martial Arts Series

Judo: Winning Ways

Jujutsu: Winning Ways

Karate: Winning Ways

Kickboxing: Winning Ways

Kung Fu: Winning Ways

Martial Arts for Athletic Conditioning: Winning Ways

Martial Arts for Children: Winning Ways

Martial Arts for Women: Winning Ways

Ninjutsu: Winning Ways

Taekwondo: Winning Ways

Kickboxing and MMA

NATHAN JOHNSON

Series Consultant
Adam James
10th Level Instructor
Founder: Rainbow Warrior Martial Arts
Director: Natl. College of Exercise Professionals

MASON CREST
www.masoncrest.com

Mason Crest Publishers Inc.
450 Parkway Drive, Suite D
Broomall, PA 19008
www.masoncrest.com

Library of Congress Cataloging-in-Publication Data on file at the Library of Congress and with the publisher

Series ISBN: 978-1-4222-3235-4
Hardcover ISBN: 978-1-4222-3239-2
E-Book ISBN: 978-1-4222-8668-5

First Edition: September 2005

Produced in association with Shoreline Publishing Group LLC

Printed and bound in the United States.

IMPORTANT NOTICE
The techniques and information described in this publication are for use in dire circumstances only where the safety of the individual is at risk. Accordingly, the publisher copyright owner cannot accept any responsibility for any prosecution or proceedings brought or instituted against any person or body as a result of the use or misuse of the techniques and information within.

Picture Credits
DollarPhotoClub: Gmg9130 67; Garrincha 68; Nicholas Piccillo 83.
Dreamstime.com: Nicholas Piccillo 6, 58, 86; MyStockPhoto88: 8; Pius Lee 18; Serghei Starus 30; Mangroove 34; Antonio Diaz 54; Radu Razvan Gheorghe: 56; ZuluPhoto: 73; Creatista: 74, 88; Bendem: 81; Nickp37: 84; Gingerciprice: 87
Paul Clifton: 11, 12, 35, 37, 62, 70.
Katie Gieratz/USAF: 34
Nathan Johnson: 32, 39, 52, 59, 64, 69.
Rogers Fund/Marie-Lan Nguyen: 78
Sporting Pictures: 17, 61.
Rogan Thomson/ActionPlusNewscom: 74
Burt Vickers: 82

Front cover image: Stace Sanchez/KickPics

Contents

Words to Understand: These words with their easy-to-understand definitions will increase the reader's understanding of the text, while building vocabulary skills.

Sidebars: This boxed material within the main text allows readers to build knowledge, gain insights, explore possibilities, and broaden their perspectives by weaving together additional information to provide realistic and holistic perspectives.

The growing popularity of mixed martial arts (MMA) evolved from the sport of kickboxing. That sport grew as a combination of several combat-oriented martial arts.

Introduction

The journey of a thousand miles begins with a single step, and the journey of a martial artist begins with a single thought—the decision to learn and train. The Martial Arts involve mental and emotional development, not just physical training, and therefore you can start your journey by reading and studying books. At the very beginning, you must decide which Martial Art is right for you, and reading these books will give you a full perspective and open this world up to you. If you are already a martial artist, books can elevate your training to new levels by revealing techniques and aspects of history and pioneers that you might not have known about.

The Mastering the Martial Arts series will provide you with insights into the world of the most well-known martial arts along with several unique training categories. It will introduce you to the key pioneers of the martial arts and the leaders of the next generation. Martial Arts have been around for thousands of years in all of the cultures of the world. However, until recently, the techniques, philosophies, and training methods were considered valuable secretes and seldom revealed. With the globalization of the world, we now openly share the information and we are achieving new levels of knowledge and wisdom. I highly recommend these books to begin your journey or to discover new aspects of your own training.

Be well.

Adam James

WORDS TO UNDERSTAND

bogu kumite Early Japanese full-contact karate
indigenous Originating in a particular region or environment
infantry Soldiers trained, armed, and equipped to fight on foot
kata Choreographed sequence of martial arts movements
krabbee-krabong A sword-, spear-, and shield-based martial art from Thailand
sparring To practice fighting
wu-shu "To stop or quell a spear"

Boxing with Kicks

Although street fighting has always had its own rules (or, more accurately, lack of rules), if we were to go back only a couple of generations in the West, we would find that kicking was not considered to be gentlemanly in a fight. Today, virtually every movie or television fight scene that lasts more than a few seconds involves kicking techniques.

Indeed, the present generation of movie-goers and martial artists expect to see kicking techniques in fights. Kicking techniques also form the basis for the martial arts movements shown in video games, illustrated in comic books, and written in books about the martial arts.

There are so many different martial arts that an accurate classification of them would be impossible. Even within a given tradition, techniques and training procedures vary from club to club and from group to group. Many martial arts, including the most modern ones, were undoubtedly inspired by martial arts from China and Japan. This includes the modern art of kickboxing. Martial arts are commonly used for entertainment purposes, but true martial arts involve much more than flashy demonstrations; their creation was for more serious

In the ring, kickboxing demands strength, flexibility, and stamina. A single kick can send an opponent flying into the ropes.

reasons, such as self-defense and personal discipline. Martial arts can be practiced by people of all ages. Training takes many forms, and can be tailored to suit differing levels of fitness and ability.

Kickboxing is a modern martial art as well as a sport. It was created by combining Western and Thai boxing techniques with other techniques drawn from a variety of more traditional Oriental martial arts, including kung fu, karate, and taekwondo.

Kung fu is a Cantonese word that can be roughly translated as "hard work." But kung fu is a really a vulgar expression for an older term, **wu-shu**. Wu-shu is comprised of two Chinese characters (ideograms): wu and shu, meaning, "to stop or quell a spear." The term "wu-shu" thus describes a Chinese form of martial art.

Karate is a Japanese word for a martial art that uses blocking, punching, striking, kicking, seizing, grappling, and throwing techniques. Karate is written using two kanji, or Japanese characters (ideograms): kara and te. Kara means "empty," and te means "hand," or "hands." The word "karate" is therefore translated as "the art of empty hands" or "the art of fighting without weapons."

Taekwondo is a Korean martial art that is, likely, based largely on Japanese and Okinawan karate. Taekwondo favors high kicks, free-**sparring** techniques, and sporting contests. In fact, modern taekwondo is an Olympic sport.

Kickboxing was established during the martial art boom of the 1970s. More eclectic and free, and far less formal than traditional Oriental martial arts, kickboxing really took off in the U.S. and the U.K., where some of the first freestyle groups were developed and established.

Unlike more conservative and traditional martial arts, kickboxing places

The American kickboxing supremos Bill "Superfoot" Wallace and Joe Lewis "eye" each other up—tongue-in-cheek fashion. Lewis and Wallace spearheaded American kickboxing. Having been hook-punched by Bill, I can vouch for why he is so successful!

no emphasis on set movements, forms, or **kata** (traditional solo choreographed sequences of movements). It is largely independent from Oriental philosophy, as well as Eastern codes of behavior and healing techniques (although Thai boxers—the Eastern form of kickboxers—do have their health monitored when they are competing).

Some claim that American karate tournament fighters became frustrated with the tournament scoring system and devised kickboxing as a full-contact alternative. In fact, kickboxing has only a few similarities to karate—and then only to a certain type of karate, called

Benny “The Jet” Urquidez doing a (very) high front kick. Everyone tried to beat him and failed! Benny still draws huge crowds—particularly among his American and Japanese fans, even though he is retired.

bogu kumite. The similarities between kickboxing and bogu kumite include the use of protective equipment and full contact. There are differences between the two, however, and one of the biggest can be found in the hand techniques. While bogu kumite uses karate punches, modern kickboxing uses Western boxing techniques, including jabs, hooks, crosses, uppercuts, and a wide range of other types of body blows.

In kickboxing, great emphasis is placed on delivering punches with full force, as is done in boxing proper. Because early kickboxing had a poor reputation for safety, the World Kickboxing Association and other regulating bodies were set up during the 1970s. Early kickboxing superstars from this era included the incomparable Joe Lewis, Bill "Superfoot" Wallis, Howard Jackson, and the unforgettable Benny "The Jet" Urquidez, possibly the most successful kickboxer ever. Movie and martial arts star Bruce Lee, while not a kickboxing competitor, had a huge influence on the techniques of the sport as well.

Martial artists are renowned for being able to defend themselves with nothing more than their bare hands. This means that they must learn to transform fists, elbows, knees, and feet into a range of practical, natural weapons. Kickboxers—perhaps even more so than other martial artists—need to cultivate extremely practical techniques because, ultimately, they may be tested in the kickboxing ring.

THAI BOXING

Thai boxing is a unique form of boxing that includes kicking techniques, grabbing and holding techniques, and tripping and sweeping techniques. There are many similarities between Eastern kickboxing

methods, such as Thai boxing, and Western kickboxing methods.

Specialty Thai boxing methods include the roundhouse kick and an extensive use of elbow and knee techniques. The elbow point and the flat of the elbow are used at close quarters to strike upwards, downwards, backwards, and horizontally. The knee is used at both long and medium ranges, as well as at close quarters. The following are some examples of Thai boxing knee techniques.

DIAGONAL KNEE STRIKE

Seizing your opponent at close quarters, grapple with him or her by grabbing his or her neck. Pulling his or her head forward onto your shoulder, execute a diagonal knee strike to your opponent's solar plexus.

FLYING KNEE STRIKE

This is an especially spectacular Thai boxing technique. Leap off the ground and lunge towards your opponent's solar plexus, chest, or head with an extended knee. Take care to protect your head when using this technique, or you may be struck while advancing.

RISING KNEE STRIKE

Your opponent has attempted a right hook. Leaning back to avoid the attack, throw forward your right hand, grasp the back of your opponent's neck, and pull him or her forward onto a rising knee strike.

THE HISTORY OF THAI BOXING

The ancestors of the Thai people originally came from China. These early settlers were driven south into the Mekong and Salween valleys

KNEE STRIKES

FLYING KNEE STRIKE: Keep well guarded while airborne to minimize the danger of counterattack.

RISING KNEE STRIKE: This tactic is a favorite of Thai boxers who use it with brutal efficiency.

during the 13th century. There, they mixed with the **indigenous** Khmer population.

It is hard to find any genuine traditional connection between early warfare in Thailand and the art of Thai boxing, known there as Muay Thai. Early Thai battles were fought between armies of **infantry** equipped with shields and helmets, and the introduction of firearms during the 16th century made many of the existing military strategies and tactics obsolete.

Thai boxing proper seems to have been cultivated in and around the social life associated with Thai religious temples. Because Thai boxing hand techniques closely resemble those of Western boxing, it is difficult to believe that Western boxing techniques were a later invention.

Ancient Thailand did possess a form of ritualized combat: a weapons system known as **krabbee-krabong,** or "sword-spear." The krabbee was a short, single-edged, curved blade. Krabbee-krabong fighters also used a round shield for protection. The combat was choreographed, but the sheer speed and ferocity of the techniques survived the centuries, and krabbee-krabong can still be seen as a martial art.

At the beginning of the 20th century, Thai boxing was taught in Siamese schools. The number of injuries sustained in training was high, however, and so the government was forced to put a stop to it. Nevertheless, Thai boxing continued to flourish, and today it can be found all over Thailand, especially in Bangkok.

Early Thai boxing was a bloody and violent affair, with no weight divisions or proper rules (although biting, hair pulling, and kicking a fallen opponent were forbidden). Thai boxing only took up the use of boxing gloves in 1929. In earlier times, fighters used to bind their hands and forearms with horsehide strips. Later, this binding was replaced with a rope made from hemp (a coarse, rope-like grass) or glue-soaked strips of cotton. According to some sources, some fighters even mixed ground glass into their bindings.

MODERN THAI BOXING

Modern Thai boxing, although more refined, is still a grueling business, and it is common for professional Thai boxers to train for five hours or more per day. Training is so severe and contests so punishing,

Even though there are rules in Thai boxing and kickboxing, contests can be punishing. Here a kickboxer successfully blocks a round kick with a combination of a raised knee and a protective forearm cover/block.

that the life expectancy of serious Thai boxers is considerably reduced, and a Thai boxer's career typically does not last more than six years or so. It is common for a Thai boxer to take as his surname the name of the camp in which he trains, to show his loyalty.

Many Thai boxers train twice a day: once in the morning and once in the afternoon. Thai boxers training for a fight undergo a medical and weight check on the morning of the fight. The fighters usually receive a long massage before the fight with special sports oil called namman

Traditional Muay Thai matches begin with a ritual prayer. Each fighter kneels facing the direction of their home or their training camp and cover their face with their gloves.

muay, which is used to increase blood circulation and to improve and enhance muscular performance.

All fights are accompanied by loud, and sometimes menacing and discordant, music. Although absent from modern Western kickboxing, ritual plays an important role in Thai boxing. Before stepping into the ring, a boxer will kneel down and engage in a short prayer. The boxer will then kneel and face the direction of his or her training camp, home, or birthplace, cover his or her eyes with his or her gloved hands, and bow low, touching the canvas three times in salutation.

Following this prayer, the boxer will perform a ritual dance called ram muay that consists of a slow shadow-boxing routine. The boxer may move around, stopping at each corner of the ring, where he or she may lower his or her head and stamp his or her foot several times to assert his or her dominance. This routine serves as a warm-up exercise, and is also a form of mental preparation.

Many Thai boxers wear a piece of cloth containing a protective charm around one upper arm. This cloth is called *kruang rang*. A boxer may also wear a piece of "sacred cord," called a *mongkol*, which belongs to his or her teacher or trainer. This cord is removed before the fight. Thai boxing fights are usually scheduled for five three-minute rounds with two one-minute breaks in between.

Thai boxers engage in fitness and stamina training. This training includes long-distance running, as well as handheld focus and punching and kicking pads. The training techniques for which Thai boxers are most famous, however, are the shin-toughening and pounding drills. Thai boxers toughen their shins by impacting them on bottles filled with sand and by kicking hanging bags filled with a variety of materials.

A TOURIST ATTRACTION

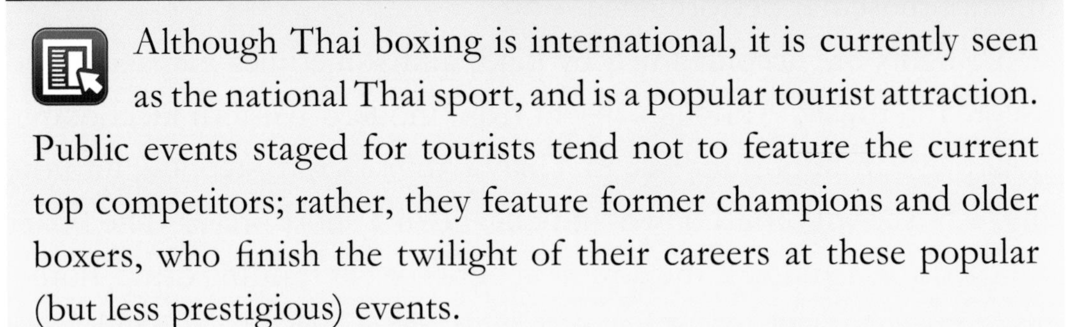
Although Thai boxing is international, it is currently seen as the national Thai sport, and is a popular tourist attraction. Public events staged for tourists tend not to feature the current top competitors; rather, they feature former champions and older boxers, who finish the twilight of their careers at these popular (but less prestigious) events.

Impacting their shins on these surfaces is designed to desensitize them to pain. These practices should not be attempted without supervision, however, as they can be extremely painful and disfiguring.

KICKING TECHNIQUES

Foot techniques expand the arsenal of natural weapons found in Thai boxing and kickboxing. Natural weapons on the foot include the ball of the foot, the top of the arch, the little toe edge of the foot, and the heel. Like its Western counterpart, kickboxing, Thai boxing has also borrowed techniques from Western boxing, kung fu, karate, and taekwondo, but one characteristic feature of Thai boxing is its distinctive and much-used roundhouse kick.

THE ROUNDHOUSE KICK

The roundhouse kick is a type of kick in which the body pivots, using the non-kicking leg as an axis. This kick differs from those found in other types of martial arts because contact is made with the shin. The kick is delivered primarily by a twisting action of the body, and

THE ROUNDHOUSE KICK

THE BENEFITS OF KICKBOXING

Kickboxing offers many benefits to those who practice it. The following list is by no means exhaustive:

- Increases confidence
- Increases fitness, strength, and flexibility
- Improves stamina
- Provides a measure of self-defense

thus the leg need not be primed to the same extent as is necessary for a karate kick. The kicking leg is held almost straight on delivery.

To perform this kick, raise your knee, lift it out to the side, and then bring it forward and across your body. Pivot the supporting leg outwards, keeping the raised leg relaxed. Continue pivoting the supporting leg until it has turned more than 90 degrees. Keeping both elbows tucked into your ribs and your chin down (to avoid any counterattack), lean your body away from the target, and then arc the kick into the target, striking with the shin.

THE FRONT KICK

The front kick is the most manageable kick to perform. Raise the knee of your kicking leg so that it is at least parallel with the floor. Make sure that the knee of the supporting, or platform, leg is well bent and that the supporting foot is pointing forward. Thrust the kicking leg out and forward while pushing the ankle forward and pulling the toes back, so that if the kick were to land, it would make contact with the ball of the foot.

THE SIDE KICK

Raise the knee of your kicking leg so that it is at least parallel with the floor. Make sure that the knee of the supporting, or platform, leg is well bent and that the supporting foot is pointing sideways. Turn your hips until the thigh of the kicking leg faces the intended target and the lead hip is in a comfortable position. Thrust the kicking leg sideways and out while bending the ankle and pulling the toes back. The point of contact is the edge of the foot.

THE FRONT KICK

Make sure you avoid "telegraphing" (letting your opponent see the kick coming). Aim the kick by pointing the knee at the target. The kick is landed using the ball of the foot as an impact point.

THE ROUND KICK

Raise the knee of your kicking leg so that it is at least parallel with the floor. Make sure that the knee of the supporting, or platform, leg is well bent and that the supporting foot is pointing sideways. Begin to turn the hip of the kicking leg as you "flick' the leg out in a semicircle.

The point of contact for this kick should be either the top of the arch or the ball of the foot.

THE BACK KICK

Pivoting on the ball of your front leg, turn your body 180 degrees. Raise the knee of your kicking leg so that it is at least parallel with the floor. Make sure that the knee of the supporting, or platform, leg is well bent and that the supporting foot is pointing directly backwards. Thrust the kicking leg out backwards, towards the target.

The point of contact for this kick should be the heel.

THE JUMPING KICK

Raise the knee of the rear leg so that the thigh is parallel with the floor. Spring off the ground with the front leg, then flick out a front kick with the rear leg, followed swiftly by a mid-air front kick with the front leg.

There are other kicks in the kickboxing repertoire, including the spinning kick, the flying side kick, the flying round kick, and the jumping-back-spinning kick. Although such kicks are popular for demonstrations, they are considered impractical for real fighting.

THE SIDE KICK

Thrust the side kick to your intended target, taking care to position your hips properly. The side kick, although appearing in several martial arts, is executed with subtle differences. For example, the side snap kick, which is quickly retracted, and the side thrust kick, which is delivered with a follow-through.

WESTERN KICKBOXING

There are two basic types of modern Western kickboxing: semi-contact, in which the combatants are only allowed to land light, controlled blows; and full-contact, in which the ultimate aim is to achieve a knockout. Individual schools and clubs hold interclub open or

THE ROUND KICK

STEP 1: Make sure that the toes of the supporting leg are turned out and away from your intended target.

STEP 2: After full extension, prepare to withdraw the kicking leg as quickly as possible to avoid getting caught by a counterattack.

invitation competitions and engage in both national and international competiti...

...ien practice kickboxing, the two sexes ...her. Combat rules differ between the ...t authorities are extremely wary of

...pected to wear protective equipment, ...elds; shin, hand, and foot pads; and ...uards for women. Western kickboxing ...egard, as Thai boxers normally only ... and gum shields.

...s from Thai boxing in that it makes ...taekwondo-type kicking techniques. ...contact kickboxing. Indeed, it is not ... boxers to wear modern karate-style ...rate belt (called an obi).

KICKING TECHNIQUES

When performing the kicking techniques of any martial art, it is important to remember that some people are naturally more flexible than others. People who are less flexible risk injury if they try to copy those who are more naturally flexible. In order to keep kicks safe, keep them as natural as possible.

In addition, pay particular attention to the knee and hip positions during the preparatory stages of a kick, particularly when executing side and round kicks. It is easy to develop strains if you are not properly warmed up.

THE BACK KICK

STEP 1: Turn to face the target quickly, but carefully. Do not strain turning your head!

STEP 2: Kick outwards and backwards as naturally as you can. Turn your body to face your target as soon as you have completed the kick.

The most effective kicks are those that are kept within the individual's natural range of movement. With practice, this range of movement can be successfully extended. However, if it is overextended, damage—or even serious injury, such as groin strain or a hernia—can result, so be careful.

THE JUMPING KICK

STEP 1: Kick forward with a middle-level front kick.

STEP 2: Launch yourself strongly into the air and prepare to extend a second kick quickly.

STEP 3: Take care to keep impact with the floor to a minimum to protect the knee joint.

WORDS TO UNDERSTAND

focus mitts Lightweight boxing gloves that protect the wearers hands from damage in sparring, and reduce the risk of cuts being inflicted on the opponent.

Kickboxing for Fitness and Fun

Modern kickboxing is used by a number of fitness clubs as a means to work out, stay in shape, and have fun. At such clubs, the confrontational or combative elements of kickboxing are reduced, and some clubs even go so far as to remove contact sparring altogether.

Kickboxing can be fun if the fitness element is stressed. You can practice the various techniques alone, in shadow-boxing fashion, or you can practice a kind of "mock sparring" with a partner, in which well-controlled (almost slow-motion) techniques are thrown, but with absolutely no contact.

The image of kickboxing has changed recently, from a sort of "spit and sawdust," nitty-gritty affair (mostly practiced by men) to a more accessible and popular recreational activity practiced by men, women, and children. Kickboxing clubs have now opened up in most major cities. Some of these clubs are open to the public, while others are private, such as college and university clubs. Private coaching is also available, with some personal fitness coaches adding kickboxing to fitness regimes constructed for individuals.

Thousands of men and women are using kickboxing as a workout tool. It's a great full-body cardio workout, while also building strength and flexibility.

KICKBOXING AND MMA

Kickboxing has become a Westernized synthesis of many existing martial arts, yet it retains its own unique character. As martial arts go, it is fluid, informal, and short on theory—particularly when compared to the esoteric types found in some other martial arts. Despite this lack of sophistication, however, kickboxing remains effective—even brutally so—and realistic in both its outlook and the practical results to come from hard, serious training.

Unlike Western boxing, Thai boxing permits (encourages!) holding and hitting. In this example, a female kickboxer controls her opponent with a neck-hold as she lands a knee strike to his solar plexus.

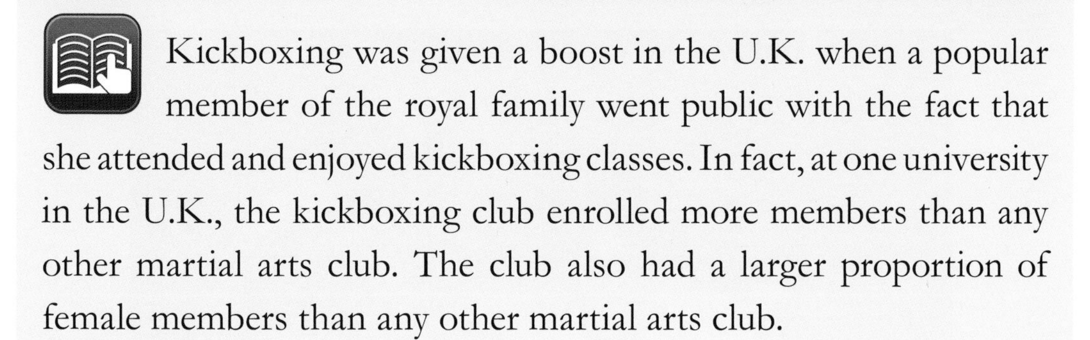

A ROYAL ENDORSEMENT

Kickboxing was given a boost in the U.K. when a popular member of the royal family went public with the fact that she attended and enjoyed kickboxing classes. In fact, at one university in the U.K., the kickboxing club enrolled more members than any other martial arts club. The club also had a larger proportion of female members than any other martial arts club.

WARMING UP

Before you can practice kickboxing, you will need to warm up. You should work towards the goal of strengthening and toning your body to keep fit and to minimize the risk of injury during training. Following are some effective exercises for warming up.

ABDOMINAL CRUNCH

Lie comfortably on the floor, raise your knees, and place your hands at the sides of your head. Raise your body as you pull your knees up

ABDOMINAL CRUNCH

Avoid doing this exercise on a full stomach. Do not try to do too may repetitions in the beginning. Start with a few and gradually work your way up.

FITNESS CRAZE

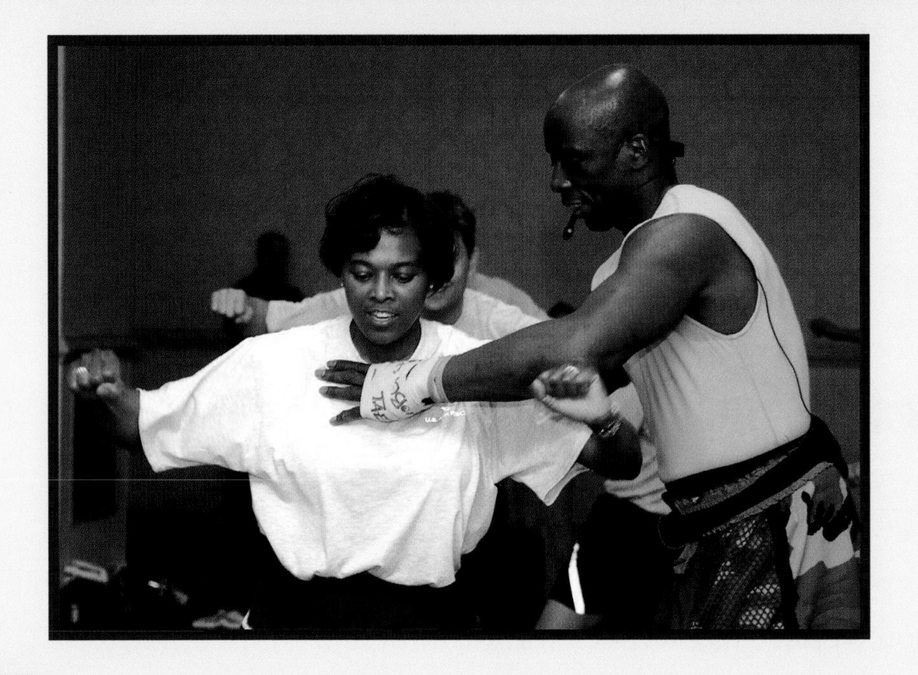

Using elements of taekwondo, karate, and other martial arts, Billy Blanks (above at right) created a national fitness craze with his Tae Bo program. A karate world champion and member of the Karate Hall of Fame, Blanks opened a fitness studio near Los Angeles in 1989. Soon, his action-packed, high-energy workouts were attracting attention from Hollywood celebrities, including dancer Paula Abdul, actor Lou Diamond Phillips, and basketball star Magic Johnson. Their interest helped him get support to create videos and other training aids. Tae Bo videos soon became a regular part of working out for millions of people of all ages and backgrounds. Blanks' skill was in merging the techniques of martial arts so that anyone could use them to exercise.

towards your chest, then lie back down, making sure that neither your feet nor your head touch the ground. Repeat several times.

HORSE STANCE AND PUNCH

Squat in a "horseback riding" stance by stretching your legs apart, keeping your back straight, and bending your knees. Thrust out alternately with your fists, holding each position for at least 30 seconds. Repeat several times.

HAMSTRING STRETCH

This exercise should be performed slowly and gently. It is designed to stretch and strengthen your hamstrings. It is important that you do not favor one leg over the other when doing this exercise.

Have a training partner take hold of your leg at the ankle (ask him or

Great flexibility is an asset in the ability to deliver kicking techniques, but remember, in a contest, you are statistically more likely to get knocked down or out by a punch.

ABDOMINAL PRESS

This exercise should be practiced with great care. Pay particular attention to spasms or twinges in your back. If you get any, do the exercise without a partner.

her to avoid putting pressure on the tendon in your heel). Your partner should squat so that you can safely place your leg on his or her shoulder, and then he or she should carefully help you stretch your leg, which you should keep straight. Try to hold the position for a minimum of six seconds, and repeat several times on each leg.

ASSISTED ABDOMINAL CRUNCH

Lie on your back, and place your hands at the sides of your body or lightly on your stomach. Spreading your legs, slow your breathing and ask your partner to gently push down on your legs towards the floor (to stretch them for you) for 20 to 30 seconds. Repeat several times. It is important to perform this exercise carefully and to not push the legs down with great force.

Landing blows on a moving target is the ultimate "litmus test" in kickboxing. You can, however, get a pretty good idea of the destructive power of your kicks by using a kicking bag. Here, a Thai boxer lands a high round kick.

SAFETY

It is important that the punching or kicking bag is properly secured, so always check its stability before you begin your practice session. You should also make sure that the bag is in good condition, so that you do not sustain any cuts or lacerations. Finally, always make sure that you are properly stretched and warmed up before using a punching or kicking bag.

ABDOMINAL PRESS

This exercise is designed to strengthen your stomach muscles. Lie on your back, and tuck your knees into your chest. Place your hands on the floor at your sides. Your partner should lean forward, resting on the soles of your feet, so there is a degree of tension between both of you. Hold this position for 10 to 20 seconds, making sure that it is not painful. Repeat several times.

TRAINING EQUIPMENT

Kickboxers make extensive use of equipment to practice focusing their blows. Training equipment includes kicking bags, punching bags, **focus mitts**, kicking shields, and speedbags.

Many types of martial arts use punching and kicking bags to help them perfect techniques. Traditional martial arts stylists often train to perfect their form by practicing techniques in the air. Modern kickboxers and full-contact fighters, however, typically spend considerable amounts of time hitting and kicking a variety of bags.

PUNCHING BAG

Punching bags are filled with a variety of different materials and range in firmness. If you are going to hit a punching bag repeatedly and powerfully with your fists, you should wear special gloves designed for this purpose. Consider having your hands bandaged prior to a heavy workout with a bag.

Bandaging the hands is an old boxing safety measure designed to prevent “knuckle spread,” a condition in which the base joints of the fingers become loosened and spread out as a result of repeated impact

When you hit a punching bag for the first time. You will most likely get a shock—your blows will probably slip or glance off the bag. It takes skill and experience to land a solid jab punch like this.

on a bag. If you are going to kick a bag, it needs to be heavy enough to provide resistance, but soft enough not to damage your legs, even after repeated impact.

Punching bags are used to develop a full range of punching techniques, including jab, cross, hook, and uppercut punches.

THE JAB PUNCH

When throwing a jab punch, the lead arm is thrust out and forward, corkscrewing or spiraling as it goes (the arm is never fully extended, however). When performing this punch, take care to slightly raise the

JAB PUNCH

STEP 1: Adopt a ready stance, watching and waiting for the right moment to throw the punch.

STEP 2: Throw out the jab and be ready to retract it the instant it lands. Make sure the returning hand is held up to protect your chin.

shoulder of the punching arm; keep the chin tucked in and the guard hand (the non- punching hand) held high, with the elbow protecting the ribs. These defensive measures offer protection against a counterattack, particularly a hook to the head. This punch is thrown from medium to long range. Targets for the jab punch include the chin, the nose, and the eyes.

CROSS PUNCH

When throwing the cross punch, be prepared to receive a counterpunch, unless you score cleanly.

THE CROSS PUNCH

This is a powerful punch that is thrown diagonally, usually using your strongest arm. It is often used in combination with the jab punch. Like the jab punch, it is thrown from medium to long range.

To throw a cross punch, thrust out the punching arm from one side of your body, so that the punch crosses an imaginary midline. When using the cross punch, be sure to keep the non-punching hand upright, with the elbow pointing down to protect the ribs and the fist near (but not touching) the jaw to protect it.

The target of this punch is usually an opponent's jaw. One of the effects of this punch is a knockout.

HOOK PUNCH

STEP 1: From a well-guarded position, prepare to "power out" a hook punch.

STEP 2: You may choose to exhale forcefully when you execute this punch. It definitely adds to the powered focus.

THE HOOK PUNCH

This is a short-power punch thrown from close range. It can be thrown with either the lead or the rear hand. To throw this punch, begin by thrusting the punching arm out and forward. After this initial movement, raise the elbow, tighten the shoulder and armpit, and land the punch with a horizontal hooking action, with the back of the knuckles facing upwards.

Delivered in a horizontal arc, this type of punch is devastating if it lands on a target with considerable force. The power of this punch derives from the fact that it is "shortened," which means that less power escapes from the elbow of the punching arm. Moreover, one theory says that the human body produces the most power through a natural curve movement (such as the one in this punch). This theory, however, runs contrary to that of modern karate, which says that the most power is produced using a straight trajectory.

THE UPPERCUT PUNCH

Like the hook punch, this is a short punch delivered from close range. Sometimes, however, it is used in an extended form as a type of "sucker" punch as a surprise-attack tactic to catch an opponent unaware.

Uppercut punches can be thrown with the lead or the rear hand. To throw this punch, arc

UPPERCUT PUNCH

This picture illustrates an uppercut thrown with the rear hand. It is one of the most devastating punches in the kickboxing arsenal.

USING FOCUS MITTS

STEP 1: If you are holding the focus mitts, make sure you hold them firmly. If you are striking the mitts, do so from a proper and well-balanced position.

STEP 2: Physics tells us that for every action, there is an equal and opposite reaction. Be prepared to accept the impact results of your strikes. A good stance is essential for this.

the punching hand upward with a crouching action. Make sure to keep the chin tucked in and the non-punching hand protecting the chin and ribs. The uppercut rises quickly from a low level to a high one. A well-thrown uppercut that snaps an opponent's head back (which frequently results in a knockout) is one of the most controversial aspects of kickboxing, Thai boxing, and Western boxing, because of the potential damage that can be caused by the punch.

FOCUS MITTS

Most modern martial arts, including kickboxing, use focus mitts. These mitts are used in conjunction with a partner in order to improve accuracy, timing, and speed. A partner holds the pads in a particular position to invite a specific technique. For example, he or she may hold the mitt pad-side to the ground to invite an uppercut punch to be thrown.

The basic angles at which the focus mitts are held are square on (for jabs), sideways (for turning kicks), and angled (for hooks). Reaction time can be improved by suddenly changing the position of the mitt so that you have to decide quickly which technique to use. Focus mitts can be used singularly or in pairs. Once you become competent at hitting a moving target with a high degree of accuracy, you will be able to put together combinations with blinding speed, a must for effective full-contact fighting.

Here is an effective practice technique using focus mitts. Have your partner stand just within your natural distance (about the length of your leg), holding either one or two focus mitts. Ask him or her to stand still at first, until you get used to landing a clean, focused blow on the mitt. Once you can do this, ask your partner to move around, changing distances while moving backwards, sideways, or even forward, to cramp your space.

USING THE KICKING BAG

Not all kickboxing is about sweat and pain. Experimenting with a kicking bag can be good and rewarding fun. And, you can find out for yourself how a particular technique works best for you! Thrust the round kick out strongly, making sure you do not bend your head forward; otherwise the impact might unbalance you.

Once your confidence and skill have increased, you could ask your training partner to launch partial attacks at you using the mitts. The purpose of these attacks is not to land a punch; they are just to provoke a reaction. Your partner might, for example, step forward and launch a light left-hooking action towards your head, completing the action by placing the focus mitt in a position that invites you to counter with a right cross punch.

KICKING BAGS

Kicking bags are filled with a variety of different materials and, like punching bags, vary in firmness from soft to hard. Typically, a more experienced practitioner would use a harder bag for training.

Two types of round kick, the Thai boxing round kick (see pp. 24 and 26) and the kickboxing round kick (see pp. 20–22), can be practiced using a kicking bag. When practicing the round kick using a kicking bag, make sure that you do not stand too close to the bag. Your supporting leg should be well bent and angled away from the bag.

Here is an effective practice technique using a kicking bag. Begin by kicking the bag lightly, performing no more than 10 kicks with each leg before changing sides. Gradually increase the pace and power of the kicks until they reach full power. Drop the pace down again after two to three minutes to allow accumulated toxins to filter out of the bloodstream (the after-burn of oxygen creates toxins that can give you a "stitch"). After a minute or so of slow tempo, increase your output to its maximum. Repeat the cycle according to your own level of fitness or according to your training program.

KICKING SHIELDS

All of the blows and kicks that can be practiced using a kicking bag can also be practiced using an air shield. Air shields come in a variety of shapes and sizes, and are usually filled with foam. They can be used to develop focus, timing, rhythm, and power. Air shields differ considerably from focus mitts because they are capable of soaking up great impact force and will tax your power reserves.

Air shields come with a variety of handles and gripping devices, and it is important to learn how to hold them properly. Failure to do so will result in the impact of the blows causing the shield to hit the person holding it (usually somewhere unpleasant, like the face). Also, improperly held air shields will prevent the blows and kicks being practiced from landing properly (they tend to slide off the air shield if it is not held correctly).

Here is an effective practice technique using an air shield. Have a partner stand in front of you, presenting a properly held air shield. Practice one blow or kick at a time until you are skillful and confident enough to put a combination or series of combinations together.

SPEEDBAGS

The speedbag is a piece of equipment borrowed from conventional boxing. It is a small, light, inflated ball about the size of a small melon. The bag is suspended at head height or just above. The speedbag is used to develop rhythm, timing, and fluidity. Using the speedbag has little to do with developing overall punching power, however, and is not struck with conventional blows.

Using a speedbag will help you develop the muscles you need to keep your hands up during sparring or in tournament fighting. A kickboxer who lets his or her guard drop will usually be struck and knocked down or out, which is why it is vital to maintain a proper guard at all times. Using the speedbag will help to cultivate and maintain this habit.

COMBINATIONS

STEP 1: Prime the knee by raising it as shown, to prepare for step 2.

STEP 2: Fully extend the leg in a round kick.

STEP 3: Follow the round kick with a jab punch.

STEP 4: Finish with a rear hand hook punch.

HOW TO STRIKE A SPEEDBAG

You will find using a speedball to be a bit tricky at first. The problem lies in trying to locate the speedbag after it has bounced off the circular board from which it is suspended. With a bit of practice, however, you will get used to it.

Stand facing the speedbag in a natural and relaxed posture. It is

USING A SPEEDBALL

Rhythm, timing, speed, and eye-hand coordination are all enhanced by using a speedball.

customary to advance the leg you would naturally put forward when shadow boxing, sparring, or using a punching bag. Raise your arms so that they are in front of the speedbag, and clench your fists. An optional move now is to twist and spiral your left fist clockwise, and your right wrist counterclockwise (this twisting motion adds a preparatory "tone" to your forearms). Letting your wrists spring back from their twisted state (if you have twisted them), punch your fists towards the speedbag, one after another, in rapid and rhythmic succession. Raise your elbows to work the muscles on the undersides of your arms (the triceps), while simultaneously working your shoulder muscles (the deltoids).

Speedbag blows should be hit with a sort of a rolling, tumbling action, with the blows landing from above the ball.

A KICKBOXING FITNESS REGIME

The following kickboxing fitness regime is given merely as an example; fitness routines are most effective when they are tailored to suit an individual. The example is based on eight categories of training: calisthenics, stretching, kicking bag work, kicking in the air, skipping, boxing bag work, shadow boxing, and running.

CALISTHENICS

You should gradually increase the number of repetitions given for each exercise. Do not worry if your friends can do more push-ups than you can, as the training should be tailored to suit your own ability.

PUSH-UPS

Lie face down on the floor with your legs slightly apart. Place the palms of your hands flat on the floor with your arms placed slightly beyond the width of your shoulders. Raise your body upwards, until your arms are straight, and then gently lower yourself down until your body almost touches the ground (your lowered body may touch the ground so long as it does not bear any weight). Do not hold your breath during this exercise.

Start with as many repetitions as you can comfortably manage and progressively build up in sets of 8 to 10 repetitions. Please bear in mind that push-ups are not an indication of general strength and that some people can naturally do more than others. Each person should, therefore, concentrate on his or her own performance. Do 5 to 10 repetitions if you are new to this exercise.

SQUAT THRUSTS

Place the palms of your hands flat on the floor with your arms placed slightly beyond the width of your shoulders. Raise your body upwards until your arms are straight. Drive forward with your knees, tucking them in and up towards your chest while maintaining your arm and upper body position. To complete one action, thrust back with your

Running is part of many sports fitness regimes, particularly combat sports like kickboxing that have a competitive basis. Be sure to wear proper running shoes if you are running on concrete, otherwise stick to softer ground.

legs until your feet are in their original position. This action should be done smoothly and carefully to avoid strain or injury. Do 10 to 15 repetitions if you are new to this exercise.

JUMP-UPS

Begin by placing the palms of your hands flat on the floor with your arms slightly beyond the width of your shoulders. Raise your body upwards until your arms are straight. Drive forward with your knees, tucking them in and up towards your chest while maintaining your arm and upper-body position. Jump or stand up quickly from the crouching position. Do five repetitions if you are new to this exercise.

CRUNCHES

This exercise concentrates on tightening and strengthening the abdominal muscles. Good control of the abdominal muscles is vital in any martial art. Crunches also help to develop stamina.

Lie flat on your back and bend your knees approximately 90 degrees. Raising your hands to the sides of your head and keeping your elbows tucked in, lift your body about 45 degrees from the floor while exhaling. Lower yourself down again as you inhale. Do 5 to 10 repetitions if you are new to this exercise.

STAR JUMPS

Starting in a natural and relaxed posture, throw your arms out and up as you jump up, spreading your legs as you do so. Jump up repeatedly, opening and closing your legs as you simultaneously throw your arms out and up to the sides.

Working on punching bags is a great way to develop not only better kicking technique, but stamina and cardio fitness.

KICKING IN THE AIR

When practicing air-kicking techniques, you should concentrate on speed. As usual, make sure that you are properly warmed up. An effective practice regime is as follows: 15 to 20 repetitions of the round kick, the side kick, and the front kick.

SKIPPING

Using a skipping rope is a popular form of exercise for building a person's overall fitness, reflexes, and levels of endurance. It is a favored means of training for most boxers. To get the most from this technique, skip for two minutes, rest, and then repeat.

BOXING BAG WORK

Using a light focus pad, practice the following techniques for two minutes on both sides: jabs, hooks, crosses, and uppercuts.

SHADOW BOXING

To practice shadow boxing, simply go through the movements or techniques you have already learned, and try to incorporate new techniques, variations, and combinations. It is also good to vary the speed, combinations, timing, and rhythms used.

Avoid full extension of your limbs when shadow boxing, as fully locking the arms or legs when practicing techniques in the air may make your knee or elbow joints ache. Taken to the extreme, this can develop into "tennis elbow" (an inflammation of the elbow joint causing pain common to racket-based sports) or inflamed tendons. To avoid such injury, keep your movements fluid, do not fully extend your limbs, and keep your movements and techniques as natural as possible. Practice on both sides for two minutes each.

THE RIGHT WAY TO STRETCH, BY ADAM JAMES

The need for a thorough warm-up before any form of exercise, no matter how gentle it may appear, cannot be overstated. A great many sports injuries can be avoided with just a few minutes of warming up. The frequent kicks and rapid changes of direction that are found in many martial arts are demanding on the joints, so particular attention should be accorded to these areas.

There is no one way of warming up, but the general rule is to move and loosen up all the major joints and muscle groups of the body. The main joints are the wrists, elbows, shoulders, ankles, knees, hips, and the spine. The major muscle groups are the hamstrings and quadriceps, the large bundles of muscles at the front and rear of the thighs; the two muscles that make up the calves; the tendon that attaches your heel to your calf (Achilles tendon); and the muscles of the arms, shoulders, back, and chest.

WARM-UP PROGRAM

Once you have changed into appropriate clothing, you are ready to warm up. There are many options for warm-up activities

including brisk walking, light jogging, bike riding, or other cardio exercise machines if available, such as a treadmill, rowing machine, elliptical machine, or stepper. Also, one can do light calisthenics like jumping jacks, lunges, etc. For the martial artist, it's effective to warm-up by gently performing katas or forms, as well as doing shadow boxing/shadow fighting.

STRETCHING

Stretching builds on the effects of the warm-up, and properly prepares the body for rigorous exercise. Proper stretching will prevent injuries and enhance peak performance. All stretches are either dynamic or static—in other words the body is either moving (dynamic) or it is not moving (static). Prior to exercise, which involves movement, it's very important to move during stretching. Dynamic stretching will allow the body to move through the range of motion for the joints and prepare it for exercise. Another principle of stretching is that all stretches are either active or passive—in other words the person is either moving the body or there is an external force that pushes the body through the range of motion. Static Passive Stretches are excellent for after exercise and can enhance range of motion; however, they can weaken muscles if done prior to exercise and diminish athletic performance. Dynamic Active Stretches are ideal before exercise and will prepare the body for movement.

Full-contact kickboxing is one of the forerunners of MMA. Anyone taking up this martial art should be fully trained and aware of the risks involved.

FULL-CONTACT FIGHTING

Full-contact is a general term that applies to karate, taekwondo, kung fu, Thai boxing, and kickboxing. Each has slightly different systems of competition; some are based on semi-contact fighting, whereas others are based on full-contact fighting.

In semi-contact fighting, kicks and punches are landed with controlled force at accepted targets, while in full-contact fighting, full-force blows and kicks are delivered. The most dangerous category of fighting is obviously full-contact because the risk of injury—particularly to the brain—is great.

The brain is a soft-tissue organ. Although the skull protects the brain in most circumstances, if the head is struck forcibly, the brain will suffer injury.

In fact, thousands of brain cells are destroyed every time the head is struck. The damage is not immediately obvious; somebody who has been repeatedly punched or kicked in the head may complain of a headache or

CAUTION

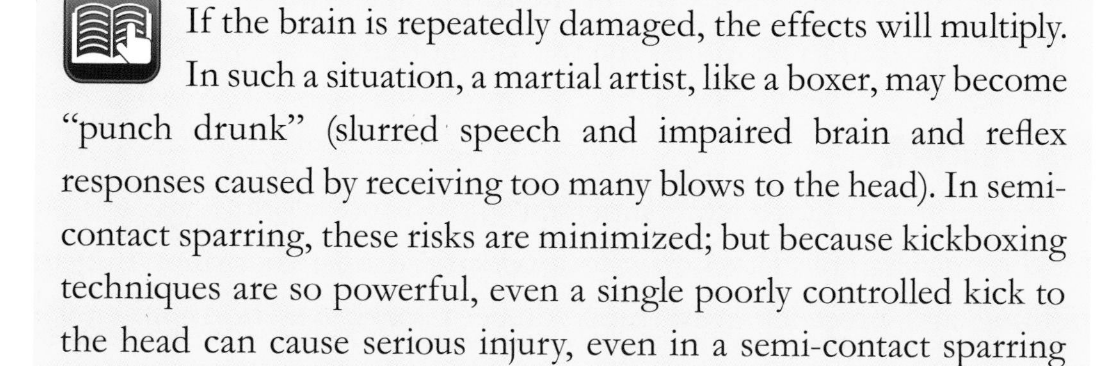

If the brain is repeatedly damaged, the effects will multiply. In such a situation, a martial artist, like a boxer, may become "punch drunk" (slurred speech and impaired brain and reflex responses caused by receiving too many blows to the head). In semi-contact sparring, these risks are minimized; but because kickboxing techniques are so powerful, even a single poorly controlled kick to the head can cause serious injury, even in a semi-contact sparring situation.

suffer from poor concentration in the short term. So long as the damage is not serious, however, recovery can take place. Of course, the wearing of headguards will dramatically reduce the level of risk.

Full-contact fighting was devised as a way of allowing all of the impact-based martial arts to compete both against themselves and against each other. Initially, there appeared to be stylistic differences between certain types of martial arts fighters (kung fu fighters and karate or taekwondo fighters, for example), but these differences later disappeared as the fighters' experience grew, and they discovered what works and what does not work in the ring.

Surprisingly, traditional techniques were less effective in the full-contact ring than had been imagined. Kicks like the "back turning" or "spinning" kick, a great scoring technique in semi-contact fighting, proved to be woefully inadequate in full-contact fighting. Moreover, when the technique failed (as it invariably did), the kicker was often punished for being caught off-balance or with his or her back turned or with his or her head and body facing away from the point of conflict. The use of punching bags also changed opinions as to what would work and what would not work in the full-contact ring, as some blows and kicks proved to be more effective than others.

FOOTWORK

According to kickboxing superstar and former world heavyweight kickboxing champion Joe Lewis, footwork is the most important thing in fighting and precedes everything. Once a kickboxer becomes quick on his or her feet, he or she can transfer this speed to punches and kicks, thereby making them powerful. Kickboxers without mobility are

Natural instincts for self-preservation and survival are heightened during kickboxing sparring. Here, the intense concentration on the faces of these kickboxers demonstrates these enhanced instincts.

ineffective because they are unable to land their punches and kicks.

Kickboxers do not move in fixed patterns. Unlike karate and other related martial arts, kickboxing does not use a full step to deliver a punch. Effective kickboxing footwork should be as natural as possible. This means that you should move your body smoothly and quickly, keeping your balance and remaining light on your feet. Avoid dancing

Despite the long range of kicking techniques, and despite the legs being approximately four times stronger than the arms, some kickboxing tournaments have to stipulate that a minimum of eight kicks must be thrown per round, because it is often difficult to land clean kicks on a moving target.

around unnecessarily. Also, never hold rigid or tense defensive positions, as these have a negative effect on the mind and will lead you to cower if you get hit. Nature provided the "fight-or-flight responses" (see p. 64). Use them.

BODY EVASION

Some kickboxers claim that the best defense is a good offense, but even this requires good positioning and the avoidance of an opponent's attack through body shifting or repositioning. Repositioning can best be understood in terms of the points of the compass. There are eight basic directions that can be taken—backwards, forwards, sideways (both ways), and any combination thereof.

Moving backwards is both natural and easy, but your opponent can continue moving forward—and can do so faster than you can move backwards. Moving sideways and backwards is an excellent tactic because it forces your opponent to readjust his or her position in order to follow you. Moving sideways and forwards is also effective, provided that you have good close-quarters skills and can neutralize any attacks. Even just going forward into an attack can be a form of evasion.

Finally, some fighters favor "tying up" another fighter's arms, entangling them and preventing the other fighter from launching a punching attack. This tactic is not quite as effective in kickboxing as it is in normal boxing, because a kickboxer can still use a leg technique, even in a "clinch."

WORDS TO UNDERSTAND

compound attack An attack that combines several different moves

Kickboxing as Self-Defense

While certain tactics can help boost your confidence, it is important not to have unrealistic expectations about what you can actually do to protect yourself in a situation—otherwise, you may find yourself in over your head. You must accurately and honestly weigh the given situation before deciding how to act.

There is a world of difference between the self-defense needs of a warrior on a battlefield and those of a child being picked on in the schoolyard. Consequently, a combat-active Marine will not receive the same training as, say, a young person taking kickboxing classes. Generally speaking, however, there are certain elements of self-defense that apply equally to all types of situations that call for it.

One of the best-known defenses of all time is already programmed into the human brain. It requires little training and is generally extremely effective. It is also a good recipe for a long life. It is called running away. Standing and fighting is something that should always be avoided unless you have no other choice.

Timing is a critical factor in the success of a kicking technique. In a tournament situation, it is quite common for both fighters to attempt to kick at the same time. When this happens, the fighter who is the quickest off the mark with a punching technique will be the most likely to score.

Good mental preparation is essential for success. A fighter should be relaxed—so as not to waste energy—and properly warmed up.

It is a mistake to be ashamed of being afraid. Fear is a natural reaction and can even be used in a positive way as part of the mental preparation for conflict. Under stress, our bodies produce a natural hormone called adrenaline. When we are faced with a challenging or threatening situation, adrenaline is pumped into the bloodstream to provide us with an energy boost. This reaction prepares us for what is known as the "fight-or-flight syndrome."

There are two consequences of fear that can affect us adversely. The first is that sometimes it can paralyze us, making us freeze and do nothing—sometimes with disastrous consequences. The second consequence of fear is that it can cause a drastic over-reaction.

IF YOU HAVE TO FIGHT

First and foremost, always try to avoid any fight in which a weapon is involved. If you are caught in a situation in which a weapon is produced, you must keep away from it at all costs. Improvise a weapon of your own, if necessary, but remember that an attacker may take your improvised weapon as a greater threat and act even more unreasonably.

You must also take into consideration the attacker's distance, timing, and the nature of the weapon concerned. For example, if you are threatened with a knife and you pick up a chair to use as a weapon, you may be able to keep an attacker at bay over the long and middle ranges. At close range, however, the chair will be next to useless.

If an attacker shows a weapon, do what you can to avoid it. Counterattacking with an improvised weapon can buy time for a retreat.

This boxer demonstrates a good defensive posture. Always keep your hands near your head.

Something else to remember is to always protect your head at all costs. If your head takes a direct hit of sufficient power, your whole body may go down—you may be knocked out. When covering up, guarding, or otherwise protecting yourself, keep your forearms tucked into your ribs, your shoulders up, and your chin tucked in. Turn in your front foot to bring your front thigh in and towards your groin to protect it. Be prepared to punch your aggressor with all the force, training, and experience at your disposal. Take care to keep properly covered up while executing your punch, and never stop looking for an opportunity to escape.

Once you have delivered a punch, be prepared to follow up. A blistering combination should be able to beat someone of your own size and strength who has little or no experience fighting, even if he or she is a bully.

PHYSICAL PREPARATION

It is important to bear in mind that while punching someone will no doubt be unpleasant for him or her, it will likewise be painful for you. You will be making contact using your (unprotected) knuckles, and thus

Children and young people can safely enjoy sparring only if they treat it as a game, and use their natural (play) instincts to control the distance—as they do in schoolyard games such as "tag."

DOUBLE COVER

When double covering, make sure that your fists do not obscure your line of vision.

you should expect to incur some sort of injury. Practicing punching using a heavy punching bag can at least prepare you for the impact. Indeed, sports science tells us that the best way to warm up for an activity is to approximate that activity as closely as possible.

It is only through constant repetition that the skills of defense and offense can be learned, sharpened, and maintained. Basic skills can be acquired in a matter of months, and reflexes can be sharpened. It is important, however, to keep it all in perspective. Remember that no one can prepare for every eventuality. It would be unwise for you to fill your head with constant thoughts about a fight that may never happen.

In modern kickboxing, preemptive striking (hitting first) is always seriously considered. But hitting someone before they hit you does raise certain moral and ethical questions. For instance, how can you be sure that the person is really

Kickboxers need to control natural instincts—like aggression—and channel them into explosive combinations and skillful defenses.

going to hit you? And even if you are relatively sure that the person is going to hit you, how do you know how hard the blow will be? It could be just a light blow that you could either tolerate or quickly escape from after it was delivered. Would the blow deserve the devastating combination that you are about to unleash on your opponent?

The final decision regarding preemptive striking rests with you, but if you can avoid it in any way, you should do so. It is always best to wait for the other person to strike out first and then defend yourself and hit back, if necessary. Also, bear in mind that if you hit someone else first, you could get into trouble with the law.

ROLLING WITH THE PUNCHES

STEP 1: Keep well covered, pivot, twist, and roll when you are attacked with a compound attack (many blows).

STEP 2: Be prepared to "spring out" from the double defensive guard with a counter-attack.

GETTING CAUGHT BY A PUNCH

STEP 1: When your opponent is close enough to be able to hit you, you should be properly covered—unlike this example.

STEP 2: And remember, your opponent's lead (front) hand is the closest to you and can reach you quickly…ouch!

A trainer holding a pad makes a great target for kickboxing workouts.

DEFENDING YOURSELF

In training to defend yourself using kickboxing, what is required is a measure of realism. In order to benefit from the training described in the following paragraphs, you will need a competent partner or trainer. You will also need appropriate equipment. This will consist of a gum shield, a head guard, a body protector, and two pairs of boxing gloves.

The idea in self-defense kickboxing training is to familiarize yourself with being physically assaulted. Facing one blow at a time is fairly simple and will instill basic confidence; however, things get trickier when facing a **compound attack**.

The skills you develop in the ring and the practice gym can come in handy if you need them for self-defense "in the street."

A compound attack is an attack consisting of an unspecified number of blows, delivered in fierce combinations that cover the full range of kickboxing techniques. Starting with a single attack (preferably by a trusty friend or an experienced coach), gradually build up the number of attacks, until you can defend yourself against a compound attack. There are a number of techniques that can be used to absorb this type of punishment without getting hurt.

Do not try to "block" each and every individual technique. Keep covered instead. Protect your jaws with your fist and your ribs with your elbows. Move your body continually in order to avoid becoming a "sitting duck." Roll with the punches, and slide back, sideways, or even forward to avoid or check kicks. Duck, bob, and weave, and be prepared to explode with a dynamic compound combination of your own when you sense an opening.

Using the double-cover guard in which both arms protect you from blows to an area from the jaw to the ribs, pivot, twist, duck, roll, and dodge to avoid a compound attack. You could also consider moving forward and inward in order to stifle attacks at the source. If you do so, however, be prepared to use short punching techniques (hooks or uppercuts, for example) to counterattack.

In training to absorb and neutralize blows in this way, you will gain valuable defensive skills that only kickboxing training can provide. You will also gain the useful experience of following up a defensive position with an immediate counterattack, which is, arguably, the most important tactic in any martial art.

WORDS TO UNDERSTAND

hybrid A mix of several similar elements to make something new

submission The act of forcing an opponent to submit, or surrender

Mixed Martial Arts

By Adam James

Mixed Martial Arts, also known simply as MMA, is a combat sport that has become very popular worldwide with both spectators and practitioners. MMA involves full contact martial arts techniques including striking, clinching, and grappling. The Ultimate Fighting Championship (UFC) is the largest professional MMA organization, and the sport is regulated by athletic commissions.

While MMA is often seen as a modern martial art/combat sport, there have been full contact contests between different martial arts styles for hundreds of years, as well as numerous martial arts masters throughout history who have blended martial arts techniques. Bruce Lee, the founder of jeet kune do, is often referred to as the Father of Mixed Martial Arts because he encouraged people to include fighting techniques from a variety of martial arts styles. Lee wrote about his philosophy of "absorb what is useful" and taught his students a blend of martial arts, which developed into a **hybrid** fighting method.

In ancient Greece, one of the original Olympic competitions was

MMA has become one of the most popular combat sports in the world, attracting big audiences to live events, as well as drawing viewers to televised action. It's an intense combination of martial arts skills of many types..

The ancient Greeks included many fighting sports in their military training, including the rough-and-tumble Pankration, pictured here on a vase.

called Pankration and it involved wrestling and striking. While this early form of Mixed Martial Arts was not included in the modern Olympics, the classical Greeks performed it in their military training, as well as the ancient Olympics and then passed it on to the Romans.

As various martial arts systems developed in Asia, there were many teachers who would advocate combining striking and grappling, while others preferred one approach. As a result, there were different styles that developed and competitions to test them against each other.

During the 19th century, as boxing was developing into a popular sport in Europe and America, there were numerous matches between boxers and wrestlers. While these weren't MMA competitions, they certainly led the way to comparing techniques and strategies.

In 1963, Gene LeBell, a judo champion and wrestler, fought Milo Savage, a professional boxer, in the first televised mixed style competition. LeBell won by a rear naked choke and he went on to become a pioneer of grappling and Mixed Martial Arts. LeBell was a Judo champion and professional wrestler, who then went on to become a Hollywood stuntman and martial arts instructor. An expert in catch wrestling, LeBell was one of the first people to use the name grappling, and he has taught many top MMA champions.

The modern sport of MMA developed in America, Japan and Brazil during the late 20th century. Bruce Lee, LeBell, Leo Fong, and other top American martial artists advocated combining martial arts and developing a free fighting approach that was not tied to any one style. In Japan, shoot wrestling was developing as a popular spectator sport. Meanwhile in Brazil, the style of Brazilian jiujitsu was developing alongside the No Holds Barred sport of Vale Tudo. The Gracie family of Brazil issued an open challenge to fight them, and this eventually led to the Ultimate Fighting Championship (UFC). Royce Gracie won the very first UFC, which had no weight classes

Gene LeBell was a judo champion who pioneered what became MMA.

Leo Fong and Bruce Lee and Their MMA Connection

Leo Fong was born in China in 1928, but moved to America in the 1930s and grew up in Arkansas and Texas, where he became a Golden Gloves, AAU and Inter-collegiate boxing champion. Fong eventually moved to the San Francisco Bay area where he achieved black belts in jujutsu and taekwondo, as well as mastered several kung fu systems including Choy Lay Fut and Sil Lum kung fu. In the 1960s, Bruce Lee and Leo Fong became close friends and training partners. Lee taught Fong his Wing Chun kung fu and Fong influenced Lee with Western boxing.

One day, Bruce Lee asked Leo Fong why he was training in so many different martial arts styles, and Fong answered that he was "looking for the ultimate." Bruce Lee replied that "the ultimate is inside of you." He went on to tell Fong that his boxing skills, combined with taekwondo kicks, kung fu and jujutsu grappling techniques was the ultimate martial art.

Leo Fong went on to write one of the very first books on combining martial arts to form one system of fighting entitled *Wei Kuen Do: The Psychodynamic Art of Free Fighting.* Fong's style of Wei Kuen Do means "the way of the integrated fist" and he advocates integrating boxing techniques and strategies with kicks and grappling. Fong also co-wrote *Power Training in Kung Fu and Karate*, one of the first books on sports-specific training with weights for the martial arts athlete.

The UFC took the sport of fighting to a new level, with national TV broadcasts and lots of press attention, as at this event for a 2012 fight.

or restrictions on techniques. During this time, the common term for these competitions was No Holds Barred or NHB, and several fighting tournaments were held under various names including Pancrase, Strikeforce, and the Pride Fighting Championship.

Eventually UFC became the leading organization and the name Mixed Martial Arts was used as the common name for the sport itself. UFC bought the rights to the other top MMA organizations and gained control of the sport. There are several other MMA competitions but the UFC is regarded as the top professional level.

KAJUKENBO: THE FIRST MODERN MIXED MARTIAL ART

Developed in the late 1940s in the Palama Settlement area of Hawaii, Kajukenbo is often regarded as the first modern mixed martial art. The system was designed specifically for street fighting, and combines the martial art styles of karate, judo/jujutsu, kenpo, kung fu/Chinese boxing, and Western boxing. Created by five of the top martial artist of Hawaii who called themselves the Black Belt Society, these men would meet and train together to share their respective knowledge and techniques. After years of dedicated work, the system was called Kajukenbo (Ka for karate; Ju for judo/jujutsu; Ken for kenpo; and Bo for Chinese and western boxing). Adriano Emperado (pictured above), the kenpo expert, became the primary leader of the organization and helped develop the style into a very popular martial art in Hawaii. Eventually, Kajukenpo spread to the mainland of the United States, and today it is practiced all over the world.

MMA TRAINING

To be a champion in the sport of MMA, the athlete must be well trained in the different aspects of fighting: striking, clinching/take downs, and grappling. The top MMA fighters must also be extremely well-conditioned athletes with excellent speed, strength, flexibility, power, and endurance. They must also be mentally focused, disciplined, and resilient.

In the early years of No Holds Barred competitions, the fighters usually were based in one specific style and strategy of fighting. For example, they were an expert in grappling or striking, but usually not both. Eventually, as the sport developed, the athletes trained to become

MMA training lets athletes with different specialties use them in fighting and sparring.

more well rounded, and like Bruce Lee had advocated decades before, they began to adopt various martial arts techniques from different styles.

MMA TECHNIQUES AND TRAINING DISCIPLINES

While MMA has developed into a single sport, the training disciplines from several martial arts systems are the keys to developing excellent techniques.

Boxing: Western Boxing punches and defensive skills such as slips are the base for almost all MMA fighters' striking techniques.

Traditional Western boxing techniques are key skills for any MMA participant.

THE ULTIMATE FIGHTER CHANGED THE SPORT

In the early years of Mixed Martial Arts, the sport faced great criticism and had a very limited fan base. Many politicians and citizen groups campaigned against the sport, and most journalists and media companies refused to cover MMA. Then in 2005, the UFC created a reality show competition called "The Ultimate Fighter" that aired on cable television. During the finals, two young MMA athletes, Forrest Griffin and Stephan Bonnar, faced off to earn a shot at a professional contract with UFC. The bout was extremely close as the evenly matched fighters went back and forth. Millions of viewers were enthralled with the competition and eventually Forrest Griffin was declared the winner. However, in a major surprise, the UFC announced that both athletes would receive the prize of a professional contract to fight with UFC. The first Ultimate Fighter show forever changed MMA and it emerged as a new major combat sport.

Brazilian Jiujitsu: Developed in Brazil from traditional Japanese jujutsu, Brazilian jiujitsu (BJJ) gained notoriety during the 1990s, as Royce Gracie won the Ultimate Fighting Championship using the Gracie Family techniques. Today, BJJ and grappling are a staple of Mixed Martial Arts training.

Judo: The throws, takedowns, chokes, and arm bars of the traditional Japanese martial art are widely used in MMA. Furthermore, many MMA champions started in judo and then eventually switched to MMA.

Karate: Classical karate often included strikes, takedowns, and basic grappling techniques such as chokes and arm bars. An excellent foundation for kickboxing and MMA, numerous karate athletes have gone on to become champions in MMA.

Kickboxing and Muay Thai: In addition to boxing, Muay Thai and Western kickboxing are often regarded as the most important foundation for MMA striking skills. Excellent kicking techniques like the roundhouse kick often lead to victory. Dynamic kicks like spinning kicks are less common in MMA but are used from time to time.

Wrestling: Olympic and catch wrestling are also very popular training disciplines for MMA athletes. In the early days of shoot wrestling in Japan, Karl Gotch, a catch wrestler, taught many of the first champions. In addition, the term No Holds Barred, which was used to describe the sport before Mixed Martial Arts became common, is a catch wrestling name for open competitions.

MMA FIGHT STRATEGIES

At the early NHB tournaments, fighters came from a variety of martial arts styles but usually fell into one of two categories in regards to strategy: strikers or grapplers. The strikers were from styles like karate and kickboxing and they preferred to not go to the ground. The grapplers came from judo, BJJ, and wrestling and they tried to grab their opponent and grapple. Today's MMA athletes are adept at both, but often prefer fighting with a specific strategy.

Ground and Pound: The fighters attempt to grab their opponent, go to the ground, and get a position of dominance. Then they will use basic strikes to achieve victory or create opening for **submission** techniques.

The ground and pound strategy places one fighter in a position of dominance over the other. Of course, women take part in MMA as well as men.

When one fighter has the other in a submission hold like this, the fight is often over soon.

Sprawl and Brawl: With this strategy, the fighter avoids going to the ground by using the sprawl, and prefers stand up striking from boxing and kickboxing.

Submission Grappling: The grappler strives to take the opponent to the ground, and then uses chokes, arm bars and leg locks to get the opponent to tap out or submit.

MMA TRAINING

Professional MMA athletes train in a variety of ways to develop speed, strength, flexibility, and endurance. The modern sports training methods include weight lifting, plyometrics, running, and cross training. In 1998, the National College of Exercise Professionals teamed up with Rainbow Warrior Martial Arts to create the first ever MMA Trainer certification program. Graduates of this course are certified as an MMA Strength & Conditioning Coach, and also as a trainer in the sport of Mixed Martial Arts.

SAFETY AND SPORT REGULATION

As with all combat sports, safety and proper training are paramount to the health of the athlete. All safety precautions must be considered prior to starting MMA training or any exercise programs. People can train in MMA for fitness benefits and never enter into a competition. Athletes who participate in an amateur or professional MMA bout must be fully prepared and use correct procedures. Over the years, Mixed Martial Arts competitions have evolved to include weight categories and now follow state and national athletic commission requirements.

GLOSSARY

Bogu kumite karate Early Japanese full-contact karate

Bout An athletic match

Compound attack An attack that combines several different moves

Dojo A Japanese term used to describe the martial arts training hall

Feint A pretend blow or attack on or toward one area in order to distract attention from the point one really intends to attack

Focus mitt A pad used in training to help a kickboxer learn to aim his or her punches and kicks

Hybrid A mix of several elements to make something new

Indigenous Originating in a particular region or environment

Infantry Soldiers trained, armed, and equipped to fight on foot

Ippon One point or score

Karate-ka A person who practices karate

Kata Choreographed sequence of martial arts movements

Krabbee-krabong A sword-, spear-, and shield-based martial art from Thailand

Kruang rang	A piece of cloth containing a protective charm worn by Thai boxers
Kyokushinkai karate	A type of Japanese knockdown, full-contact karate
Mongkol	A piece of "sacred" cord belonging to a Thai boxing teacher or trainer and worn by a fighter
Parry	To evade or ward off a weapon or a blow
Ram muay	A ritual dance conducted by Thai boxers before a fight
Shihan	A Japanese term used to recognize one of the highest grades of martial arts, that of master
Spar	To practice fighting
Submission	The act of forcing an opponent to submit, or surrender
Surname	A person's last name
Wu-shu	This means "to stop or quell a spear."

Clothing and Equipment

Clothing

Gi: The gi is the most typical martial arts "uniform." Usually in white, but also available in other colors, it consists of a cotton thigh-length jacket and calf-length trousers. Gis come in three weights: light, medium, and heavy. Lightweight gis are cooler than heavyweight gis, but not as strong. The jacket is usually bound at the waist with a belt.

Belt: Belts are used in the martial arts to denote the rank and experience of the wearer. They are made from strong linen or cotton and wrap several times around the body before tying. Beginners usually wear a white belt, and the final belt is almost always black.

Hakama: A long folded skirt with five pleats at the front and one at the back. It is a traditional form of clothing in kendo, iaido, and jujutsu.

WEAPONS

Bokken: A bokken is a long wooden sword made from Japanese oak. Bokken are roughly the same size and shape as a traditional Japanese sword (katana).

Jo: The jo is a simple wooden staff about 4–5 ft (1.3–1.6 m) long and is a traditional weapon of karate and aikido.

Kamma: Two short-handled sickles used as a fighting tool in some types of karate and jujutsu.

Tanto: A wooden knife used for training purposes.

Hojo jutsu: A long rope with a noose on one end used in jujutsu to restrain attackers.

Sai: Long, thin, and sharp spikes, held like knives and featuring wide, spiked handguards just above the handles.

Tonfa: Short poles featuring side handles, like modern-day police batons.

Katana: A traditional Japanese sword with a slightly curved blade and a single, razor-sharp cutting edge.

Butterfly knives: A pair of knives, each one with a wide blade. They are used mainly in kung fu.

Shinai: A bamboo training sword used in the martial art of kendo.

Iaito: A stainless-steel training sword with a blunt blade used in the sword-based martial art of iaido.

TRAINING AIDS

Mook yan jong: A wooden dummy against which the martial artist practices his blocks and punches and conditions his limbs for combat.

Makiwara: A plank of wood set in the ground used for punching and kicking practice.

Focus pads: Circular pads worn on the hands by one person, while his or her partner uses the pads for training accurate punching.

PROTECTIVE EQUIPMENT

Headguard: A padded, protective helmet that protects the wearer from blows to the face and head.

Joint supports: Tight foam or bandage sleeves that go around elbow, knee, or ankle joints and protect the muscles and joints against damage during training.

Groin protector: A well-padded undergarment for men that protects the testicles and the abdomen from kicks and low punches.

Focus mitts: Lightweight boxing gloves that protect the wearers hands from damage in sparring, and reduce the risk of cuts being inflicted on the opponent.

Chest protector: A sturdy shield worn by women over the chest to protect the breasts during sparring.

Further Reading

Buller, Debz and Jennifer Lawler. *Kickboxing for Women.* Wish Publishing, 2012

Delavier, Frederic. *Delavier's Mixed Martial Arts Anatomy.* Human Kinetics, 2013
Note: The author shows the muscles that are worked in MMA and kickboxing, plus exercises to strengthen them.

D'Souza, Brian. *Pound for Pound: The Modern Gladiators of Mixed Martial Arts.* Thracian Publishing, 2013

Heath, Adam T. *Mixed Martial Arts' Most Wanted: The Top 10 Book of Crazy Combat, Great Grappling, and Sick Submissions.* Potomac Books, Inc., 2011

Slipchenko, Maxim. *Thai Boxing for You: Muay Thai from a World Champion's Perspective.* Amazon Digital Services (Ebook), 2014
Note: Author is a three-time world champion in the sport.

Sobie, Brian and Adam Segal. *MMA Now! The Stars and Stories of Mixed Martial Arts.* Firefly Books, 2014.

About the Author

Nathan Johnson holds a 6th-dan black belt in karate and a 4th-degree black sash in traditional Chinese kung fu. He has studied martial arts for 30 years and holds seminars and lectures on martial arts and related subjects throughout the world. He teaches zen shorindo karate at several leading universities in the U.K. His previous books include Zen Shaolin Karate and Barefoot Zen. He lives in Hampshire, England.

Useful Web Sites

General Martial Arts information

http://martialarts.org

Ultimate Fighting Championship

www.ufc.com

Find a Kickboxing Gym Near You

http://www.gymticket.com/kickboxing/

World Kickboxing League

http://www.wklkickboxing.com

Series Consultant

Adam James is the Founder of Rainbow Warrior Martial Arts and the Director for the National College of Exercise Professionals. Adam is a 10th Level Instructor of Wei Kuen Do, Chi Fung, and Modern Escrima, and a 5th Degree Black Belt in Kempo, Karate, Juijitsu, and Kobudo. He is also the co-creator of the NCEP-Rainbow Warrior Martial Arts MMA Trainer certification program, which has been endorsed by the Commissioner of MMA for the State of Hawaii and by the U.S. Veterans Administration. Adam was also the Director of World Black Belt, whose Founding Members include Chuck Norris, Bob Wall, Gene LeBell, and 50 of the world's greatest martial artists. In addition, Adam is an actor, writer and filmmaker, and he has performed with Andy Garcia, Tommy Lee Jones, and Steven Seagal. As a writer, he has been published in numerous martial arts books and magazines, including *Black Belt*, *Masters Magazine*, and the *Journal of Asian Martial Arts*, and he has written several feature film screenplays.

INDEX

References in italics refer to illustration captions